A NIP IN THE AIR

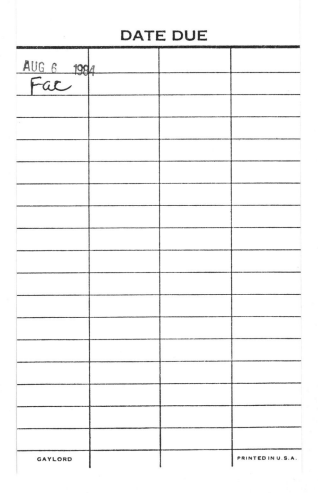

DATE DUE

AUG 6 1984 Fac			
GAYLORD			PRINTED IN U.S.A.

A NIP
IN THE AIR

John Betjeman

W·W·NORTON & COMPANY INC·
New York

Library of Congress Cataloging in Publication Data

Betjeman, John, Sir, 1906-
  A nip in the air.
  I. Title
PR6003.E77N5   1974   821'.9'12   75-28059
ISBN 0-393-04415-7
ISBN 0-393-04423-8 pbk.

Printed in the United States of America

1 2 3 4 5 6 7 8 9

Contents

Acknowledgements

The author is grateful to H.R.H. The Prince of Wales for his gracious permission to print 'A Ballad of the Investiture' and to Thomas Edward Neil Driberg again for his consistent encouragement and constructive help. He thanks the editors of *The Architect, The Cornhill Magazine, Encounter, The London Magazine, The Saturday Book, The Sunday Express* where some of the poems were first published.

To my Grandchildren
Lucy, Imogen
and Endellion

A NIP IN THE AIR

On Leaving Wantage 1972

I like the way these old brick garden walls
Unevenly run down to Letcombe Brook.
I like the mist of green about the elms
In earliest leaf-time. More intensely green
The duck-weed undulates; a mud-grey trout
Hovers and darts away at my approach.

From rumpled beds on far-off new estates,
From houses over shops along the square,
From red-brick villas somewhat further out,
Ringers arrive, converging on the tower.
Third Sunday after Easter. Public ways
Reek faintly yet of last night's fish and chips.
The plumes of smoke from upright chimney-pots
Denote the death of last week's Sunday press,
While this week's waits on many a step and sill
Unopened, folded, supplements and all.

Suddenly on the unsuspecting air
The bells clash out. It seems a miracle
That leaf and flower should never even stir

In such great waves of medieval sound:
They ripple over roofs to fields and farms
So that ' the fellowship of Christ's religion '
Is roused to breakfast, church or sleep again.

From this wide vale, where all our married lives
We two have lived, we now are whirled away
Momently clinging to the things we knew—
Friends, footpaths, hedges, house and animals—
Till, borne along like twigs and bits of straw,
We sink below the sliding stream of time.

On a Painting by Julius Olsson R.A.

Over what bridge-fours has that luscious sea
    Shone sparkling from its frame of bronzéd gold
    Since waves of foaming opalescence roll'd
One warm spring morning, back in twenty-three,
All through the day, from breakfast-time till tea,
    When Julius Olsson, feeling rather cold,
    Packed up his easel and, contented, stroll'd
Back to St. Ives, its fisher-folk and quay.

Over what bridge-parties, cloche-hat, low waist,
    Has looked that seascape, once so highly-prized,
    From Lenygon-green walls, until, despised—
" It isn't art.   It's only just a knack "—
    It fell from grace.   Now, in a change of taste,
See Julius Olsson slowly strolling back.

Beaumaris
December 21, 1963

Low-shot light of a sharp December
  Shifting, lifted a morning haze:
Opening fans of smooth sea-water
  Touched in silence the tiny bays:
In bright Beaumaris the people waited—
  This was Laurelie's day of days.

At the northern end of the street a vista
  Of sunlit woodland; and south, a tower;
Across the water from Hansom's terrace,
  The glass'd reflection of Penmaenmawr:
High on her balcony Laurelie Williams
  Waved the shovel and shot the shower.

Down on us all fell heated ha'pence,
  Up to her all of us looked for more:
Laurelie Williams, Laurelie Williams—
  Lovelier now than ever before

With your straight black hair and your fresh

                        complexion:

Diamond-bright was the brooch you wore.

Life be kind to you, Laurelie Williams,

  With girlhood over and marriage begun:

Queuing for buses and rearing children,

  Washing the dishes and missing the fun,

May you still recall how you flung the coppers

  On bright Beaumaris in winter sun.

[It was a Christmas-tide custom at Beaumaris, Anglesey, for
the Queen of the Hunt Ball to throw heated halfpence from a
shovel to the crowd below.]

Hearts Together

How emerald the chalky depths
    Below the Dancing Ledge!
We pulled the jelly-fishes up
    And threw them in the hedge
That with its stones and sea-pink tufts
    Ran to the high cliff edge.

And lucky was the jelly-fish
    That melted in the sun
And poured its vitals on the turf
    In self-effacing fun,
Like us who in each others' arms
    Were seed and soul in one.

O rational the happy bathe
    An hour before our tea,
When you were swimming breast-stroke, all
    Along the rocking sea

14

And, in between the waves, explain'd
  The Universe to me.

The Dorset sun stream'd on our limbs
  And scorch'd our hinder parts:
We gazed into the pebble beach
  And so discussed the arts,
O logical and happy we
  Emancipated hearts.

Aldershot Crematorium

Between the swimming-pool and cricket-ground
  How straight the crematorium driveway lies !
And little puffs of smoke without a sound
  Show what we loved dissolving in the skies,
Dear hands and feet and laughter-lighted face
And silk that hinted at the body's grace.

But no-one seems to know quite what to say
  (Friends are so altered by the passing years):
" Well, anyhow, it's not so cold today "—
  And thus we try to dissipate our fears.
' *I am the Resurrection and the Life* ':
Strong, deep and painful, doubt inserts the knife.

The Newest Bath Guide

Of all the gay places the world can afford,
By gentle and simple for pastime ador'd,
Fine balls, and fine concerts, fine buildings, and springs,
Fine walks, and fine views, and a thousand fine things
(Not to mention the sweet situation and air),
What place, my dear mother, with Bath can compare?

Christopher Anstey: THE NEW BATH GUIDE, 1766

It is two hundred years since he got in his stride
And cantered away with *The New Bath Guide.*
His spondees and dactyls had quite a success,
And sev'ral editions were called from the press.
That guidebook consisted of letters in rhyme
On the follies and fashions of Bath at the time:

I notice a quiver come over my pen
As I think of the follies and fashions since then. . . .

Proud City of Bath with your crescents and squares,
Your hoary old Abbey and playbills and chairs,

17

Your plentiful chapels where preachers would preach
(And a different doctrine expounded in each),
Your gallant assemblies where squires took their daughters,
Your medicinal springs where their wives took the waters,
The terraces trim and the comely young wenches,
The cobbled back streets with their privies and stenches—
  How varied and human did Bath then appear
  As the roar of the Avon rolled up from the weir.

In those days, no doubt, there was not so much taste:
But now there's so much it has all run to waste
In working out methods of cutting down cost—
So that mouldings, proportion and texture are lost
In a uniform nothingness. (This I first find
In the terrible ' Tech ' with its pointed behind.)
Now houses are ' units ' and people are digits,
And Bath has been planned into quarters for midgets.
  Official designs are aggressively neuter,
  The Puritan work of an eyeless computer.

Goodbye to old Bath! We who loved you are sorry
They're carting you off by developer's lorry.

In Memory of George Whitby, Architect

Si monumentum requiris . . . the church in which we are
                                                sitting,
Its firm square ceiling supported by fluted Corinthian
                                                columns
In groups of three at the corners, its huge semi-circular
                                                windows
Lighting the elegant woodwork and plaster panels and
                                                gilding:
Look around you, behold the work of Nicholas Hawksmoor.

Si monumentum requiris . . . not far away and behind us
Rises the dome of Saint Paul's, around it a forest of steeples
In Portland stone and in lead, a human and cheerful
                                                collection,
Mostly by Christopher Wren, Nicholas Hawksmoor's master.
Si monumentum requiris . . . at the western gate of the City
Behold the Law's new fortress, ramparting over the Bailey
In cream-coloured clear-cut ashlar on grim granitic
                                                foundations—

But, like all good citizens, paying regard to its neighbours,
Florid baroque on one side, plain commercial the other.

This is your work, George Whitby, whose name to-day we
remember:
From Donald McMorran and Dance to Wren and Nicholas
Hawksmoor,
You stand in a long tradition; and we who are left salute you.

[Delivered at Saint Mary Woolnoth, 29 March 1973.]

Delectable Duchy

Where yonder villa hogs the sea
Was open cliff to you and me.
The many-coloured cara's fill
The salty marsh to Shilla Mill.
And, foreground to the hanging wood,
Are toilets where the cattle stood.
The mint and meadowsweet would scent
The brambly lane by which we went;
Now, as we near the ocean roar,
A smell of deep-fry haunts the shore.
In pools beyond the reach of tides
The Senior Service carton glides,
And on the sand the surf-line lisps
With wrappings of potato crisps.
The breakers bring with merry noise
Tribute of broken plastic toys
And lichened spears of blackthorn glitter
With harvest of the August litter.

Here in the late October light
See Cornwall, a pathetic sight,
Raddled and put upon and tired
And looking somewhat over-hired,
Remembering in the autumn air
The years when she was young and fair—
Those golden and unpeopled bays,
The shadowy cliffs and sheep-worn ways,
The white unpopulated surf,
The thyme- and mushroom-scented turf,
The slate-hung farms, the oil-lit chapels,
Thin elms and lemon-coloured apples—
Going and gone beyond recall
Now she is free for " One and All."*

One day a tidal wave will break
Before the breakfasters awake
And sweep the cara's out to sea,
The oil, the tar, and you and me,
And leave in windy criss-cross motion
A waste of undulating ocean
With, jutting out, a second Scilly,
The isles of Roughtor and Brown Willy.

*The motto of Cornwall.

22

The Costa Blanca

Two sonnets

SHE

The Costa Blanca ! Skies without a stain !
Eric and I at almond-blossom time
Came here and fell in love with it. The climb
Under the pine trees, up the dusty lane
To Casa Kenilworth, brought back again
Our honeymoon, when I was in my prime.
Good-bye democracy and smoke and grime:
Eric retires next year. We're off to Spain !

We've got the perfect site beside the shore,
Owned by a charming Spaniard, Miguel,
Who says that he is quite prepared to sell
And build our Casa for us *and*, what's more,
Preposterously cheaply. We have found
Delightful English people living round.

HE (five years later)

       Mind if I see your *Mail* ?   We used to share

       Our *Telegraph* with people who've returned—

       The lucky sods !   I'll tell you what I've learned:

       If you come out here put aside the fare

       To England. *I'd* run like a bloody hare

       If I'd a chance, and how we both have yearned

       To see our Esher lawn. I think we've earned

       A bit of what we had once over there.

       That Dago caught the wife and me all right !

       Here on this tideless, tourist-littered sea

       We're stuck. You'd hate it too if you were me:

       There's no piped water on the bloody site.

       Our savings gone, we climb the stony path

       Back to the house with scorpions in the bath.

Lenten Thoughts of a High Anglican

Isn't she lovely, ' the Mistress ' ?
    With her wide-apart grey-green eyes,
The droop of her lips and, when she smiles,
    Her glance of amused surprise ?

How nonchalantly she wears her clothes,
    How expensive they are as well !
And the sound of her voice is as soft and deep
    As the Christ Church tenor bell.

But why do I call her ' the Mistress '
    Who know not her way of life ?
Because she has more of a cared-for air
    Than many a legal wife.

How elegantly she swings along
    In the vapoury incense veil;
The angel choir must pause in song
    When she kneels at the altar rail.

The parson said that we shouldn't stare
  Around when we come to church,
Or the Unknown God we are seeking
  May forever elude our search.

But I hope the preacher will not think
  It unorthodox and odd
If I add that I glimpse in ' the Mistress '
  A hint of the Unknown God.

[This is about a lady I see on Sunday mornings in a London
church.]

Executive

I am a young executive.　No cuffs than mine are cleaner;
I have a Slimline brief-case and I use the firm's Cortina.
In every roadside hostelry from here to Burgess Hill
The *maîtres d'hôtel* all know me well and let me sign the bill.

You ask me what it is I do.　Well actually, you know,
I'm partly a liaison man and partly P.R.O.
Essentially I integrate the current export drive
And basically I'm viable from ten o'clock till five.

For vital off-the-record work—that's talking transport-
                                                    wise—
I've a scarlet Aston-Martin—and does she go ?　She flies !
Pedestrians and dogs and cats—we mark them down for
                                                    slaughter.
I also own a speed-boat which has never touched the water.

She's built of fibre-glass, of course.   I call her ' Mandy
                                                                                        Jane '
After a bird I used to know—No soda, please, just plain—
And how did I acquire her ?   Well to tell you about that
And to put you in the picture I must wear my other hat.

I do some mild developing.   The sort of place I need
Is a quiet country market town that's rather run to seed.
A luncheon and a drink or two, a little *savoir faire*—
I fix the Planning Officer, the Town Clerk and the Mayor.

And if some preservationist attempts to interfere
A ' dangerous structure ' notice from the Borough Engineer
Will settle any buildings that are standing in our way—
The modern style, sir, with respect, has really come to stay.

Meditation on a Constable Picture

Go back in your mind to that Middlesex height
Whence Constable painted the breeze and the light
As down out of Hampstead descended the chaise
To the wide-spreading valley, half-hidden in haze:

The slums of St. Giles's, St. Mary'bone's farms,
And Chelsea's and Battersea's riverside charms,
The palace of Westminster, towers of the Abbey
And Mayfair so elegant, Soho so shabby,

The mansions where lilac hangs over brown brick,
The ceilings whose plaster is floral and thick,
The new stucco terraces facing the park,
The odorous alleyways, narrow and dark,

The hay barges sailing, the watermen rowing
On a Thames unembanked which was wide and slow-flowing,
The street-cries rebounding from pavements and walls
And, steeple-surrounded, the dome of St. Paul's.

29

No market nor High Street nor square was the same
In that cluster of villages, London by name.
Ere slabs are too tall and we Cockneys too few,
Let us keep what is left of the London we knew.

A Wembley Lad

To every ducal palace
  When days were old and slow,
Me and my sister Alice
  By charabanc would go.

My new position such is
  In halls of social fame
That many a duke and duchess
  I know by Christian name

Belvoir, Blenheim, Chatsworth,
  Luncheon, dinner, tea,
And stay the night—ah !—*that's* worth
  All the world to me.

And as for sister Alice
  She would not like it here:
She'd be nervous in a palace
  And call the duchess ' dear '.

So I'm off to the Bath Assembly
With head and heart held high
But palaceless Alice in Wembley
Knows how alone go I.

County

God save me from the Porkers,
 God save me from their sons,
Their noisy tweedy sisters
 Who follow with the guns,
The old and scheming mother,
 Their futures that she plann'd,
The ghastly younger brother
 Who married into land.

Their shots along the valley
 Draw blood out of the sky,
The wounded pheasants rally
 As hobnailed boots go by.
Where once the rabbit scampered
 The waiting copse is still
As Porker fat and pampered
 Comes puffing up the hill.

"A left and right !   Well done, sir !
    They're falling in the road;
And here's your other gun, sir."
    " Don't talk.   You're here to load."
He grabs his gun, not seeing
    A thing but birds in air,
And blows them out of being
    With self-indulgent stare.

Triumphant after shooting
    He still commands the scene,
His Land Rover comes hooting
    Beaters and dogs between.
Then dinner with a neighbour,
    It doesn't matter which,
Conservative or Labour,
    So long as he is rich.

A *faux-bonhomme* and dull as well,
    All pedigree and purse,
We must admit that, though he's hell,
    His womenfolk are worse.
Bright in their county gin sets
    They tug their ropes of pearls

And smooth their tailored twin-sets
  And drop the names of earls.

Loud talk of meets and marriages
  And tax-evasion's heard
In many first-class carriages
  While servants travel third.
" My dear, I have to spoil them too—
  Or who would do the chores ?
Well, here we are at Waterloo,
  I'll drop you at the Stores."

God save me from the Porkers,
  The pathos of their lives,
The strange example that they set
  To new-rich farmers' wives
Glad to accept their bounty
  And worship from afar,
And think of them as county—
  County is what they are.

Greek Orthodox

To the Reverend T. P. Symonds

What did I see when first I went to Greece ?
Shades of the Sixth across the Peloponnese.
Though clear the clean-cut Doric temple shone
Still droned the voice of Mr Gidney on;
" That ὅτι ?   Can we take its meaning here
Wholly as interrogative ? "   Edward Lear,
Show me the Greece of wrinkled olive boughs
Above red earth; thin goats, instead of cows,
Each with its bell; the shallow terraced soil;
The stone-built wayside shrine; the yellow oil;
The tiled and cross-shaped church, who knows how old
Its ashlar walls of honey-coloured gold?
Three centuries or ten ?   Of course, there'll be
The long meander off to find the key.

The domed interior swallows up the day.
Here, where to light a candle is to pray,
The candle flame shows up the almond eyes

Of local saints who view with no surprise
Their martyrdoms depicted upon walls
On which the filtered daylight faintly falls.
The flame shows up the cracked paint—sea-green blue
And red and gold, with grained wood showing through—
Of much-kissed ikons, dating from, perhaps,
The fourteenth century. There across the apse,
Ikon- and oleograph-adorned, is seen
The semblance of an English chancel screen.

" With *oleographs* ? " you say. " Oh, what a pity !
Surely the diocese has some committee
Advising it on taste ? " It is not so.
Thus vigorously does the old tree grow,
By persecution pruned, watered with blood,
Its living roots deep in pre-Christian mud,
It needs no bureaucratical protection.
It is its own perpetual resurrection.
Or take the galleon metaphor—it rides
Serenely over controversial tides
Triumphant to the Port of Heaven, its home,
With one sail missing—that's the Pope's in Rome.

Dilton Marsh Halt

Was it worth keeping the Halt open,
    We thought as we looked at the sky
Red through the spread of the cedar-tree,
    With the evening train gone by ?

Yes, we said, for in summer the anglers use it,
    Two and sometimes three
Will bring their catches of rods and poles and perches
    To Westbury, home to tea.

There isn't a porter.   The platform is made of sleepers.
    The guard of the last up-train puts out the light
And high over lorries and cattle the Halt unwinking
    Waits through the Wiltshire night.

O housewife safe in the comprehensive churning
    Of the Warminster launderette !
O husband down at the depot with car in car-park !
    The Halt is waiting yet.

And when all the horrible roads are finally done for,
　　And there's no more petrol left in the world to burn,
Here to the Halt from Salisbury and from Bristol
　　Steam trains will return.

Loneliness

The last year's leaves are on the beech:
    The twigs are black; the cold is dry;
To deeps beyond the deepest reach
    The Easter bells enlarge the sky.
O ordered metal clatter-clang !
Is yours the song the angels sang ?
You fill my heart with joy and grief—
Belief !   Belief !   And unbelief . . .
    And, though you tell me I shall die,
    You say not how or when or why.

Indifferent the finches sing,
    Unheeding roll the lorries past:
What misery will this year bring
    Now spring is in the air at last ?
For, sure as blackthorn bursts to snow,
Cancer in some of us will grow,
The tasteful crematorium door
Shuts out for some the furnace roar;
    But church-bells open on the blast
    Our loneliness, so long and vast.

40

Back from Australia

Cocooned in Time, at this inhuman height,
 The packaged food tastes neutrally of clay.
 We never seem to catch the running day
But travel on in everlasting night
With all the chic accoutrements of flight:
 Lotions and essences in neat array
 And yet another plastic cup and tray.
" Thank you *so* much. Oh no, I'm quite all right".

At home in Cornwall hurrying autumn skies
 Leave Bray Hill barren, Stepper jutting bare,
  And hold the moon above the sea-wet sand.
The very last of late September dies
 In frosty silence and the hills declare
  How vast the sky is, looked at from the land.

The Manor House, Hale, near Liverpool

In early twilight I can hear
    A faintly-ticking clock,
While near and far and far and near
    Is Liverpool baroque.

And when the movement meets the hour
    To tell it, stroke by stroke,
" Rococo," says the pendulum,
    " Baroque, baroque, baroak."

Encrusted vases crowd the hall,
    Dark paintings grace the stairs
And from the wild wind's harp withal
    Sound soft Lancastrian airs.

On a bend sable three garbs or—
    Th'achievements hold my gaze;
Though fierce without the tempests roar
    The banner scarcely sways.

O'er Mersey mud and Mersey flood,
 Rust-red above the holly
How trimly rides the brick façade,
 As flimsy as a folly.

The Manor House, the Green, the church—
 From Runcorn to West Kirby
You will not find howe'er you search
 So sweet a *rus in urbe*.

Shattered Image

" . . . and that you did with said intent procure
the aforesaid Sidney Alexander Green
being at the time a minor. . . ."   Aleco—
He always was just " Aleco " to me,
The shy turn of the head, the troubled eyes,
The freckled stubbiness, the curve of thigh,
Nape of the neck—my trusting Aleco.

Amateur typing by a constable
Filled in the gaps along official buff.

An after-door-chime silence.   Strawberry pink
This leadless glaze and yet I can't be sick,
And strawberry pink the basin and the bath.
In bathrooms people often kill themselves.
And this new flat is such a good address—
One-seven Alvarez Cloister, Double-you-one,
(No need to put in Upper Berkeley Street):
Under-floor heating, pale green wall-to-wall,

Victoriana in the sitting-room.
Mother insisted on the powder-blue.

When Charlie got the maximum two years
He said the lack of privacy was the worst—
Having two others with you, boring talk,
Racing and football, and the dreadful stench
From that filled bucket all the bloody night.
Of course they found out why he was inside—
And that's a thing they never will forgive,
Touching the little children, better pooves
Or murderers, they said.   I didn't touch—
Well not in the way that Charlie used to do—
". . . and that you did with said intent procure. . . ."
How many Tuinal have I got left?
Will twenty do it ?   But I mustn't try,
Especially now that I'm a Catholic.

"It is the thoughts, my son, that lead to acts
Which cry to heaven for vengeance.
Ye'll try to put those wicked thoughts away,
Ye're truly sorry for them, aren't ye now ?
God in His mercy sent ye here to me.
But British justice—Oi can't help ye there.

Let me have word of where they're sending you.
Oi'll tell the Catholic chaplain.   Holy Church
Never deserts her sons.   Your penance now. . . ."

O Holy Mary !   What will Mother say ?
She takes the *Standard* and the *Daily Mail.*

Now let me see, let me have time to think,
What have I done that they could get me for ?
Who could have talked?   And when, and where . . .
                                        and what?
Look at it calmly.   What can they really prove ?
What is the worst that Aleco could have said ?
And will they take his word against my own ?
I'm only charged—the case unproven still;
I'm innocent until they've proved the charge.
They must have set a trap for him, the brutes.
Who could have set it ?   Not his brother Jim.
He came to Minehead with us in July.
The mother ?   No.   She couldn't have.   She's a pet.
As for the father—well, he doesn't count.
Never trust women, though.   I'll ring up George.

"What rotten luck, what really rotten luck!
And if I could, you know I'd help you, Rex.

But frankly this is not a case for me.
I'm in another purlieu of the law,
Conveyancing.   It's rather as if you asked
An obstetrician to do a dentist's job—
Not that we don't respect each other's skills.
I'll give you my advice for what it's worth
And that's, get hold of a solicitor.
Maybe your family man is not the one
To whom you'd really want to spill the beans.
Well, try another.   Who did Charlie use ?
It doesn't matter whether he got off
Or whether he didn't, Rex.   The law's the law.
A lot depends upon the Magistrates.
They may dismiss the case.   On the other hand
They may commit you, or you may be fined.
All sorts of things can happen. . . (That's the child—
Olivia's left me here to baby-sit.
It makes me hanker after bachelor days.)
So I must go. . . . Good luck—and keep in touch."

"Good God, not that, but this is serious.
Who says you've done it ?   Have they any proof ?
Now look here, Rex, I've known you long enough,
Since we were kids in fact, and I will swear

47

You never could have done a thing like that,
Who's had the cheek—no, damned malicious spite—
To make this filthy charge ?   By God, old Rex,
Eileen and I have always looked to you
As someone, somehow, who was different.
I mean, you never fooled about with tarts.
I said to Eileen just the other night
'Some people don't need what we need, old girl.
Perhaps,' I said, 'if I'd not played around
I might have made the running—look at Rex,
Started from scratch, now top executive;
And look at me, still trailing on behind!
Of course it takes all sorts to make a world
And God knows *what* we do when we get pissed
But honestly I've never been so pissed
I couldn't tell a woman from a man.'
Look here old man, you've been so good to me—
Remember how we went to Ambleside
And slept the night on Dollywagon Pike ?
I wouldn't have dared to do it on my own.
Remember camp at Camber, and your friend—
That funny chap so keen on railway trains ?
And then the Major, I forget his name,
Who asked us to his house in Italy ?

48

But look here Rex, d'you really mean to say
You did it stone-cold sober ?   Are you sure ?
What was his age ?   Good God, man, let me think. . . .
We all have somewhere where we draw the line
And frankly I must draw the line at that.
I'll tell you one thing, Rex, I give my word
Eileen shall never hear of this from me.
I'd like a day or two to think it out.
Just now I simply feel inclined to puke.
I'm sorry I must go.   No, let me pay."

"D'you like a slice of lemon with it?   Good.
Look here, I'm awfully sorry about this.
Douglas has told me, and I thought it best
To have a private word with you myself.
You see, it's very awkward.   Usually
I never interfere with private life.
Live and let live, and, well, your life's your own.
I'd never take a prudish line myself,
Although that sort of thing is not my taste—
But you're intelligent and civilized.
Now had you been the porter or a clerk
It wouldn't have mattered much.   But then, you see
Our business is—well simply what it's called,

Public Relations.   And our image counts
Not with our clients only, but beyond
In the hard world where men are selling things.
And with the sort of bloke we're dealing with,
Frankly, we can't afford the sort of slur
A case like yours brings with it.
I much appreciate your work for us,
Your contacts and the valuable accounts
That may have stayed with us because of you.
I know you'll understand me when I say
This isn't personal.   I have to think
Of all your colleagues and our clients too.
We've got some tough competitors.   I'll leave
The ball in your court now, and I suggest
Instead of letting me ask you to resign
You send a note to *me*, in which you say
That resignation is your own idea
And unconnected with your work for us—
Something quite neutral which will not reflect
Any discredit upon either side.
Good luck, goodbye.   And would you, on your way
Please tell Miss Wood to bring me in my mail."

A Ballad of the Investiture 1969

The moon was in the Cambridge sky
  And bathed Great Court in silver light
When Hastings-Bass and Woods and I
  And quiet Elizabeth, tall and white,
With that sure clarity of mind
Which comes to those who've truly dined,
  Reluctant rose to say good-night;
And all of us were bathed the while
In the large moon of Harry's* smile.

Then, sir, you said what shook me through
  So that my courage almost fails:
" I want a poem out of you
  On my Investiture in Wales."
Leaving, you slightly raised your hand—
" And that ", you said, " is a command."
  For years I wondered what to do

* The Reverend H. A. Williams, then Fellow and Dean
of Chapel of Trinity College, Cambridge, now a monk of
the Community of The Resurrection, Mirfield.

And now, at last, I've thought it better
To write a kind of rhyming letter.

Spring frocks, silk hats at morning's prime,
   One of a varied congregation
I glided out, at breakfast time,
   With Euston's Earl from Euston Station,
Through Willesden's bleak industrial parts,
Through Watford on to leafy Herts
   Bound for a single destination.
Warwicks and Staffs were soaked in rain;
So was the open Cheshire plain.

The railway crossed the river Dee
   Where Mary called the cattle home,
The wide marsh widened into sea,
   The wide sea whitened into foam.
The green Welsh hills came steeply down
To many a cara-circled town—
   Prestatyn, Rhyl—till here were we,
As mountains rose on either hand,
Awed strangers in a foreign land.

I can't forget the climbing street
  Below Caernarvon's castle wall,
The dragon flag, the tramp of feet,
  The gulls' perturbed, insistent call,
Bow-windowed house-fronts painted new,
Heads craning out to get a view,
  A mounting tension stilling all—
And, once within the castle gate,
The murmuring hush of those who wait.

Wet banners flap.   The sea mist clears.
  Colours are backed by silver stone.
Moustached hereditary peers
  Are ranged in rows behind the throne.
With lifted sword the rites begin.
Earl Marshal leads the victims in.
  The Royal Family waits alone.
Now television cameras whirr
Like cats at last induced to purr.

You know those moments that there are
When, lonely under moon and star,
  You wait upon a beach?
Suddenly all Creation's near

53

And complicated things are clear,
  Eternity in reach !
So we who watch the action done—
A mother to her kneeling son
  The Crown of office giving—
Can hardly tell, so rapt our gaze
Whether but seconds pass or days
  Or in what age we're living.

You knelt a boy, you rose a man.
And thus your lonelier life began.

14 November, 1973

Hundreds of birds in the air
   And millions of leaves on the pavement,
And Westminister bells ringing on
   To palace and people outside—
And all for the words ' I will '
   To love's most willing enslavement.
All of our people rejoice
   With venturous bridegroom and bride.

Trumpets blare at the entrance,
   Multitudes crane and sway.
Glow, white lily in London,
   You are high in our hearts today !

A Mind's Journey to Diss

Dear Mary,

    Yes, it will be bliss
To go with you by train to Diss,
Your walking shoes upon your feet;
We'll meet, my sweet, at Liverpool Street.
That levellers we may be reckoned
Perhaps we'd better travel second;
Or, lest reporters on us burst,
Perhaps we'd better travel first.
Above the chimney-pots we'll go
Through Stepney, Stratford-atte-Bow
And out to where the Essex marsh
Is filled with houses new and harsh
Till, Witham pass'd, the landscape yields
On left and right to widening fields,
Flint church-towers sparkling in the light,
Black beams and weather-boarding white,
Cricket-bat willows silvery green
And elmy hills with brooks between,

Maltings and saltings, stack and quay
And, somewhere near, the grey North Sea;
Then further gentle undulations
With lonelier and less frequent stations,
Till in the dimmest place of all
The train slows down into a crawl
And stops in silence. . . . Where is this ?
Dear Mary Wilson, this is Diss.

Fruit

Now with the threat growing still greater within me,
  The Church dead that was hopelessly over-restored,
The fruit picked from these yellowing Worcestershire
  What is left to me, Lord ?   [orchards

To wait until next year's bloom at the end of the garden
  Foams to the Malvern Hills, like an inland sea,
And to know that its fruit, dropping in autumn stillness,
  May have outlived me.

Inland Waterway

He who by peaceful inland water steers
Bestirs himself when a new lock appears.
Slow swing the gates: slow sinks the water down;
This lower Stratford seems another town.
The meadows which the youthful Shakespeare knew
Are left behind, and, sliding into view,
Come reaches of the Avon, mile on mile,
Church, farm and mill and lover-leaned-on stile,
Till where the tower of Tewkesbury soars to heaven
Our homely Avon joins the haughty Severn.
Sweet is the fluting of the blackbird's note,
Sweet is the ripple from the narrow boat.

Your Majesty, our friend of many years,
Confirms a triumph now the moment nears:
The lock you have re-opened will set free
The heart of England to the open sea.

[Declaimed at the opening of the Upper Avon at Stratford in the presence of the Queen Mother and Robert Aickman, founder of the Inland Waterways Association, on 1st June, 1974.]

For Patrick, ætat: LXX*

How glad I am that I was bound apprentice
To Patrick's London of the 1920s.
Estranged from parents (as we all were then),
Let into Oxford and let out again,
Kind fortune led me, how I do not know,
To that Venetian flat-cum-studio
Where Patrick wrought his craft in Yeoman's Row.

For Patrick wrote and wrote. He wrote to live:
What cash he had left over he would give
To many friends, and friends of friends he knew,
So that the ' Yeo ' to one great almshouse grew—
Not a teetotal almshouse, for I hear
The clink of glasses in my memory's ear,
The spurt of soda as the whisky rose
Bringing its heady scent to memory's nose
Along with smells one otherwise forgets:
Hairwash from Delhez, Turkish cigarettes,

* Patrick Balfour, 3rd Baron Kinross, b. 1904.

The reek of Ronuk on a parquet floor
As parties came cascading through the door:
Elizabeth Ponsonby in leopard-skins
And Robert Byron and the Ruthven twins,
Ti Cholmondeley, Joan Eyres Monsell, Bridget Parsons,
And earls and baronets and squires and squarsons—
" Avis, it's *ages*! . . . Hamish, but it's *aeons* . . . "
(Once more that record, the Savoy Orpheans).

Leader in London's preservation lists
And least Wykehamical of Wykehamists:
Clan chief of Paddington's distinguished set,
Pray go on living to a hundred yet!

The Last Laugh

I made hay while the sun shone.
    My work sold.
Now, if the harvest is over
    And the world cold,
Give me the bonus of laughter
    As I lose hold.